MY VERY FIRST
BOOK OF

BIBLE
HEROES

Published in Nashville, Tennessee, by Oliver-Nelson Books, a division of Thomas Nelson, Inc., Publishers and distributed in Canada by Word Communications, Ltd., Richmond, British Columbia.

The Bible version used in this publication is THE NEW KING JAMES VERSION. Copyright © 1979, 1980, 1982, Thomas Nelson, Inc., Publishers.

Printed in the United States of America.

Library of Congress Cataloging-in-Publication Data

Hollingsworth, Mary, 1947–
     My very first book of Bible heroes / Mary Hollingsworth: illustrated by Rick Incrocci.
        p.   cm.
   Summary: Retells the Bible stories of such heroes as Noah, Miriam, Samson, and Paul.
   ISBN 0-8407-9230-1
   1. Bible—Biography—Juvenile literature. 2. Bible stories,
`English. [1. Bible stories.] I. Incrocci, Rick, ill. II. Title.
BS551.2.H623   1993
220.9'505—dc20   93-7292
                                                        CIP
                                                        AC

2 3 4 5 6 — 98 97 96 95 94

MY VERY FIRST BOOK OF

BIBLE HEROES

Mary Hollingsworth

Illustrated by
Rick Incrocci

OLIVER
NELSON

THOMAS NELSON PUBLISHERS
Nashville

Dear Parents,

Who is your child's hero? Is it Barney the purple dinosaur? Maybe it's Wonder Woman or Batman or Big Bird. Perhaps it's even one of your own childhood heroes, such as Mickey Mouse or the Lone Ranger.

Well, those are fun make-believe heroes all right. But the heroes of the Bible are even better. The heroes your child will learn about in this book were real people— God's people. And there stories are true, not make-believe.

Your child will like this book about God's heroes. You'll probably find one or two heroes your child will want to be like. It might be Solomon, the wisest man who ever lived. Or it might be David, who killed a lion. It might be Esther, the queen who saved her people, or Deborah, who led her people into battle.

No matter which Bible hero your child chooses to be like, you can have confidence that she or he has chosen one of God's heroes, too. The adventure stories of His amazing heroes are waiting to challenge and encourage your child. Just turn the page.

Mary Hollingsworth

Noah

The Man Who Pleased God

A flood was coming. God told Noah to build a giant boat. It was to be big enough for two of every kind of animal on earth. Noah built the big boat just the way God said. That made God happy. So God saved Noah's family and all the animals from the Flood. Noah was a real hero.

A Real Hero

1. Why was God pleased with Noah? (Noah obeyed God.)
2. Will God be pleased with you if you obey Him? (Yes.)

Noah found grace in the eyes of the LORD.
Genesis 6:8

Abraham

The Man Who Was Father of a Nation

Abram was a good man. God promised to give Abram a big family. Abram believed God. So he did just what God said to do. God kept His promise. He gave Abram many children and grandchildren. They are called Hebrews. They were God's chosen people. Then God changed Abram's name to Abraham. Abraham means "father of a nation."

A Real Hero

1. Point to Abraham's family in the picture.
2. Does God always keep His promises? (Yes.)

God said to Abraham, "I will make you a great nation."

Genesis 12:2

15

Jacob

The Man Who Wrestled with God

One night God came and wrestled with Jacob. They wrestled all night long. Then God said, "Let Me go; it is almost morning." Jacob said, "No. I will not let You go until You bless me." So God blessed him. Jacob had wrestled with God without dying. He was a real hero!

A Real Hero

1. Where is Jacob in the picture?
2. How do you sometimes wrestle with God?

Jacob was left alone; and a Man wrestled
with him until the breaking of day.

Genesis 32:24

Joseph

The Man Who Was a Prince from a Pit

Joseph had ten big brothers. But his father liked Joseph best. This made his brothers angry. So they hid Joseph in a deep pit. Then they sold him to men going to Egypt. Things looked bad for Joseph. God had a surprise for him. He made Joseph a prince in Egypt!

A Real Hero

1. Should brothers and sisters get angry with each other? (No.)
2. Put on your bathrobe. Pretend you are a prince like Joseph.

The LORD was with Joseph, and he was a
successful man.

Genesis 39:2

19

Jochebed

The Woman Who Was a Brave Mother

A woman named Jochebed had a baby boy. She was afraid the king would hurt her baby. So she hid him in a tiny basket in the river. Soon the king's daughter found the baby. She took him home to be her baby. She named him Moses. He grew up as the king's grandson. He became a great leader! Jochebed was a brave and wise mother.

A Real Hero

1. Where is baby Moses in the picture?
2. Ask an adult to help you read the story of Jochebed and baby Moses in Exodus 2.

And when she [Jochebed] saw he was a
beautiful child, she hid him three months.

Exodus 2:2

21

Miriam

The Woman Who Was a Leader of Praise

Miriam was so happy! God saved her people from the army of Egypt. God made a dry path through the Red Sea for them to walk on. Miriam wanted to show God how thankful the people were. So she led all the women in a dance to praise God.

A Real Hero

1. Why is Miriam so happy in the picture?
   (God saved her people.)
2. Make up a happy dance for God.
   Do it right now.

Sing to the LORD, for He has triumphed gloriously!

Exodus 15:21

23

Moses

The Man Who Was God's Lawgiver

Moses did what God said to do all his life. So God chose Moses for a big job. He led God's people out of Egypt. He led them to the land God promised them. God gave Moses a special law for the people to obey. We call it the Law of Moses. The Ten Commandments are part of that law.

A Real Hero

1. Why is Moses a hero? (He did what God said to do.)
2. How can you be a hero, too? (By obeying God.)

He [the LORD] gave Moses two tablets . . .
of stone, written with the finger of God.

Exodus 31:18

25

Rahab

The Woman Who Was a Friend of God's Spies

God told His people to capture the city of Jericho. So they sent two men to spy out the city. The spies stayed at Rahab's house. She knew they were God's spies. So she hid them from the king of Jericho's soldiers. She told the soldiers that the spies were gone. It was a brave thing to do. God's people came to capture Jericho. But they rescued Rahab's family.

A Real Hero

1. What do you think Rahab is telling the spies? ("You can hide over here.")
2. Put on a disguise. Pretend you are one of God's spies.

Then the woman [Rahab] took the two
men and hid them.

Joshua 2:4

27

Deborah

The Woman Who Was a Judge
and an Army Leader

Deborah was a wise woman. She was also a great leader of God's army. One day she told Barak to lead ten thousand soldiers into battle. Barak said, "If you will go with me, I will go; but if you will not go with me, I will not go!" So Deborah led the army with him. They beat the enemy! Deborah was a real hero for God.

A Real Hero

1. Pretend you are Deborah or Barak. Lead God's army into battle.
2. Sing the song "I'm in the Lord's Army."

And the children of Israel came up to her [Deborah] for judgment.

Judges 4:5

Samson

The Man Who Was God's Strongest

Samson was the strongest man who has ever lived. He was strong because he obeyed God. God helped him. One day some men tied Samson up with two strong ropes. Then he heard a thousand enemies coming. Samson broke the ropes easily. Then he beat the enemy soldiers all by himself. He was a superhero for God.

A Real Hero

1. Where did Samson get his strength? (From God.)
2. Name the strongest heroes you know. Samson was even stronger than they are.

And the Spirit of the LORD came mightily upon him [Samson].

Judges 14:6

Ruth

The Woman Who Was Loyal and Kind

Ruth's husband died. But she would not leave her husband's mother, Naomi, all alone. She took care of Naomi. She worked hard. She picked up grain for them to eat. Everyone knew how loyal and kind Ruth was. Boaz was a relative of Naomi. He asked Ruth to marry him. She did. Then they were all very happy.

A Real Hero

1. Does God want us to be loyal and kind? (Yes.)
2. Ask an adult to help you find the name of Ruth and Boaz's baby in Ruth 4:17.

Boaz said to Ruth, "All the people of my town know that you are a virtuous woman."

Ruth 3:11

Hannah

The Woman Who Was a Promise Keeper

Hannah was sad. She wanted a baby boy. But she did not have one. She prayed to God for a son. She promised the boy would serve God all his life. God gave Hannah a baby boy named Samuel. Hannah was so happy! When Samuel was old enough, Hannah kept her promise to God. She took Samuel to the temple. He grew up serving God.

A Real Hero

1. Why was Hannah a hero to God? (She kept her promise.)
2. How can you be a hero like Hannah? (By keeping promises.)

Then she [Hannah] made a vow and said,
". . . if you will give [me] a male child, then I
will give him to the LORD all the days of his life."
1 Samuel 1:11

David

The Man Who Had God's Heart

David was a shepherd. He took care of his father's sheep. One time a lion came to attack the sheep. David fought the lion. He killed it to protect the sheep. David wanted to be like God. He wanted to be good. God loved David very much. His heart was good and pure like God's heart.

A Real Hero

1. Why did God love David so much? (David had a good and pure heart.)
2. Draw your own picture of David fighting the lion.

The LORD has sought for Himself a man
[David] after His own heart.

1 Samuel 13:14

Jonathan

The Man Who Was a Best Friend

Jonathan was David's best friend. Jonathan's father was King Saul. Saul wanted to hurt David. Jonathan helped David escape from the king. He shot an arrow to signal David. It was a brave thing to do. David loved Jonathan. He was a real hero.

A Real Hero

1. Who is your best friend?
2. Read the story of how Jonathan saved David in 1 Samuel 20.

Now Jonathan loved . . . [David] . . . as he loved his own soul.

1 Samuel 20:17

39

Abigail

The Woman Who Was Wise

Abigail's husband, Nabal, was not a wise man. King David asked Nabal to feed God's soldiers. Nabal would not do it. Abigail was a wise woman. She took food to King David. She begged him not to kill Nabal. David liked Abigail. He did what she asked. Later Nabal died. David asked Abigail to be his wife. Abigail became queen.

A Real Hero

1. Ask an adult to help you fix a basket of food. Then give it to someone as Abigail did.
2. Have you ever been a peacemaker like Abigail?

So Abigail . . . followed the messengers of David and became his wife.

1 Samuel 25:42

41

Solomon

The Man Who Was God's Wisest

Solomon was the king of God's people. He loved God. He wanted to do right. God said, "Ask Me for anything, and I'll give it to you." Solomon could have asked for money or great power. He asked God to make him wise so he could lead God's people well. This made God happy. He made Solomon the wisest man who ever lived. He also gave him great power and lots of money.

A Real Hero

1. If God told you to ask for anything you want, what would you ask for?
2. Talk to God right now. Ask Him to make you wise like Solomon.

God gave Solomon wisdom and . . . great understanding.

1 Kings 4:29

Elijah

The Man Who Rode the Wind

Elijah was one of God's special messengers. He told God's message to people for many years. That made him a hero. One day Elijah and his friend Elisha were walking by a river. All at once a chariot and horses made of fire came between them. A great wind swooped down. It took Elijah to heaven. So Elijah never died.

A Real Hero

1. What do you think it would be like to ride the wind?
2. Draw a picture of the chariot and horses made of fire.

Elijah went up by a whirlwind into heaven.

2 Kings 2:11

Esther

The Woman Who Was a Brave Queen

Esther was queen of Persia. One day Haman tricked the king. The king made a law to kill all of God's people, the Jews. Esther was a Jew! The king could kill anyone who came to see him without being invited. Esther bravely went to see the king. She asked him to save her people. The king loved Esther. He welcomed her and saved the Jews.

A Real Hero

1. Make a paper crown to wear. Pretend you are Queen Esther or the king.
2. Have you ever had to do something that really scared you?

I will go to the king, which is against the law; and if I perish, I perish!

Esther 4:16

47

Job

The Man Who Was a Patient Servant of God

Job was one of God's best servants. He did everything right. He was good. Then Satan attacked Job. He killed all of Job's children. He killed Job's sheep and cattle. He made Job lose all his money. But Job loved God and trusted Him. He was a patient servant of God. God loved Job very much.

A Real Hero

1. What would you say to Job when all the bad things happened to him?
2. Why did God love Job? (He trusted God.)

[Job] was blameless and upright, and one
who feared God and shunned evil.

Job 1:1

49

Jeremiah

The Man Who Spoke for God

Jeremiah was a brave messenger for God. God was sad because His people did not obey Him anymore. He showed Jeremiah all the bad things the people did. Jeremiah cried in front of the people to show them God's sadness. This made the people angry. They tried to hurt Jeremiah. But God kept him safe. Jeremiah still spoke for God.

A Real Hero

1. Do you think God cries when you do something bad? (Yes.)
2. How can you keep God smiling? (By being good.)

God said to Jeremiah, "I have put My words in your mouth."

Jeremiah 1:9

51

Daniel

The Man Who Was God's Dream Teller

The king could not sleep. A bad dream kept him awake. He called his magicians and star watchers. He asked them what his dream meant. They could not tell him. God helped Daniel see the king's dream. Daniel told the king all about his dream. Then he told him what it meant. The king believed in God. God made Daniel ruler over all the wise men in the kingdom.

A Real Hero

1. Tell about a dream you had.
2. What do you think your dream means?

Then the secret [dream] was revealed to Daniel in a night vision.

Daniel 2:19

53

Mary

The Woman Who Was
Mother of the Lord

Mary obeyed God's laws all her life. She was pure and right. God chose Mary for a special honor. She was the mother of God's Son! The baby was born one night in a stable. A new star in the sky told the world about the baby. Mary named the baby Jesus. He was going to be the King of all the earth!

A Real Hero

1. Sing "Silent Night" with your mom or dad.
2. Why did God choose Mary to be the mother of His Son? (Because she was pure and right.)

The virgin shall be with child, and bear a Son.

Matthew 1:23

Jesus

The Man Who Was God's Son

Jesus was the most special person ever born. That is because His Father was God. Jesus did wonderful things called miracles. He made sick people well. He made dead people live again. He made blind people see. Jesus was really God in a human's body. That is why He can save us from sin. Jesus is the greatest hero of all!

A Real Hero

1. What can you do to help people?
2. Sing "Jesus Loves Me."

Call His name Jesus, for He will save His people from their sins.

Matthew 1:21

John the Baptist

The Man Who Was God's Voice in the Desert

John the Baptist lived in the desert. He ate locusts and wild honey. He wore clothes made of camel's hair. God gave John an important job. John told people that Jesus was coming soon. He told them to turn away from their sins. He said to get ready for Jesus.

A Real Hero

1. Pretend you are John the Baptist. Stand up and preach to the people.
2. Ask an adult to fix you a snack made with honey like John the Baptist ate.

John the Baptist came preaching in the wilderness.

Matthew 3:1

Peter

The Man Who Walked on Water

Jesus' followers were on a boat. The wind blew. The boat rocked. Then Peter thought he saw a ghost! It was really Jesus. He was walking on the water. Peter asked Jesus to let him walk on the water, too. Jesus said, "Come." Peter got out of the boat. He walked toward Jesus on the water. He was a brave man!

A Real Hero

1. Draw a picture of Peter walking on the water toward Jesus.
2. Read this story in Matthew 14:22-33.

When Peter had come down out of the
boat, he walked on the water to go to Jesus.
Matthew 14:29

61

Luke

The Man Who Was God's Writer

Luke was a doctor. He was also Jesus' friend. God gave Luke a job. He wrote the story of Jesus' life. This book is called Luke. It tells how Jesus was born, lived, died, and came back to life. Luke also wrote the book of Acts. It is about Jesus' church and how it grew. Thanks to Luke, we know about Jesus and His church. He is a hero.

A Real Hero

1. Sing "Tell Me the Story of Jesus" with someone.
2. Put on something white. Pretend you are Doctor Luke and help sick people.

It seemed good to me . . . to write to you
an orderly account.

Luke 1:3

A Poor Widow

The Woman Who Was a True Giver

One day Jesus sat in the temple. He watched people give money to God. Rich people gave lots of money. They had lots of money left. Then a poor woman gave two tiny coins. Jesus said she gave more than all the others. She gave all her money. She even gave her food money. She trusted God to take care of her.

A Real Hero

1. Why was the poor woman a hero? (She trusted God to care for her.)
2. Do you have something you would like to give to God?

Jesus said, "This poor widow has put in more than all."

Luke 21:3

65

Andrew

The Man Who Was a Loving Brother

Andrew heard John the Baptist teach about Jesus. He knew Jesus could save people. He knew Jesus was the Son of God. Andrew found his brother Simon (Peter). He brought Simon to Jesus. Simon was saved, too. Andrew was a loving brother. He and Simon followed Jesus all their lives. What a hero!

A Real Hero

1. How can you be like Andrew? (By telling a brother or sister about Jesus.)
2. Are you a loving brother or sister?

[Andrew] first found his own brother Simon and said to him, "We have found the Messiah."

John 1:41

John the Apostle

The Man Who Was the Lord's Best Friend

It was the saddest day ever. Jesus was on the cross. Jesus' best friend, John, stood close to Jesus' mother. They were sad. Jesus asked John to take care of His mother. He wanted John to treat Mary as his own mother. He did. John was Jesus' best friend.

A Real Hero

1. Would you like to be Jesus' best friend?
2. How can you be Jesus' best friend?

Then He said to [John], "Behold your mother."

John 19:27

69

Mary Magdalene

The Woman Who Was a True Follower

Mary Magdalene was a true follower of Jesus Christ. She loved Him. She followed Him everywhere. Mary was sad when Jesus died. She visited His tomb in the garden. But Jesus' tomb was empty! She ran to tell His other followers. Jesus chose Mary as the first person to see Him alive again.

A Real Hero

1. Pretend you are Mary. What will you say to Jesus in the garden?
2. Ask an adult to help you plant a tree in your yard. Let it remind you of the garden where Jesus was buried.

Mary Magdalene came and told the
disciples that she had seen the LORD.

John 20:18

71

Barnabas

The Man Who Was a People Booster

Barnabas was a man everyone loved. He made other people feel good. One time Barnabas sold some of his land. He gave that money to the apostles. They used it to help other Christians. Barnabas was a people booster! He was a real hero.

A Real Hero

1. Why was Barnabas a hero? (He helped people.)
2. You can be a people booster, too! Make a card for someone who needs to be cheered up.

Joses was also named Barnabas by the
apostles (which [means] Son of Encourage-
ment).

Acts 4:36

73

Stephen

The Man Who Was a Powerful Preacher

Stephen was a brave Christian. He was also a great preacher. Some people did not like what he said. They wanted to kill him. Stephen still preached the Word of God. One day a crowd threw stones at Stephen. He died. He was a hero because he loved God more than he loved himself.

A Real Hero

1. Find a small stone. Use it to remember how much Stephen loved God.
2. How can you be like Stephen? (By bravely telling others about Jesus.)

Stephen . . . did great wonders and signs among the people.

Acts 6:8

Philip

The Man Who Was a Traveling Teacher

An angel told Philip to go to the city of Gaza. On the way to Gaza, Philip met a man in a chariot. The man was reading God's Word. He asked Philip to help him understand it. Philip taught the man about Jesus. He also taught him how to be saved. The man was baptized. Then he was happy!

A Real Hero

1. Why was Philip a hero to the man in the chariot? (He told him how to be saved.)
2. Pretend to drive a chariot on the way to Gaza.

Then Philip . . . preached Jesus to him.
Acts 8:35

Dorcas

The Woman Who Was a Good Neighbor

Dorcas was a kind woman. She made coats to keep her neighbors warm. People loved Dorcas. One day Dorcas got sick and died. All the people she had helped were upset. God helped Peter bring Dorcas back to life. Then the people were happy. Dorcas was their hero.

A Real Hero

1. Draw a picture of a coat you would like to wear. Color it with your favorite colors.
2. Write a note to thank someone who did something nice for you.

Dorcas . . . was full of good works and
charitable deeds which she did.

Acts 9:36

Cornelius

The Man Whom God Heard

Cornelius was an important army leader. He loved God. He was kind. He gave gifts to others. He prayed to God often. One day God heard Cornelius' prayer. He sent an angel to Cornelius. The angel told Cornelius to send for Peter. When Peter came, Cornelius and his family were all saved.

A Real Hero

1. Ask an adult to help you write a letter to God. Thank Him for hearing your prayers.
2. Sing "Thank You, Lord" with someone.

[Cornelius] . . . who feared God . . . gave
. . . to the people, and prayed to God always.

Acts 10:2

Lydia

The Woman Who Was the First Believer in Europe

One day Paul went to the river. He saw some women praying. He sat down to teach them. One woman was Lydia. She sold purple cloth to make a living. God helped her believe Paul's preaching. She was saved and baptized that day. She was the first person saved in Europe.

A Real Hero

1. Why was Lydia a hero to God? (She was the first believer in Europe.)
2. Pretend you sell purple cloth. How will you get people to buy it?

Lydia . . . was a seller of purple. . . . The
Lord opened her heart to heed the things
spoken by Paul.

Acts 16:14

Priscilla

The Woman Who Was a
Partner in Truth

Priscilla and Aquila were wife and
husband. They were partners for God.
Apollos came to preach in their town. He
was a great speaker. He taught God's Word
the right way. But there were some things
Apollos did not know. So Priscilla and
Aquila taught Apollos more about God's
Word. Then others could be saved.

A Real Hero

1. Ask someone to be your partner. Tell
   someone about God.
2. Work with a partner to put together a
   jigsaw puzzle.

When Aquila and Priscilla heard him
[Apollos], they . . . explained to him the way
of God more accurately.

Acts 18:26

Paul

The Man Who Could Do Miracles

The apostle Paul was a great hero among God's people. He preached God's Word. He did many wonderful miracles. He healed sick people. He helped people who were crippled walk. He helped people who were blind see. He also wrote many books of the Bible. Many people learned about Jesus from Paul. They were saved. He was a great man of God.

A Real Hero

1. God loves you as much as He loved Paul. What will you do for God?
2. What can you do to help a person who needs it?

Now God worked unusual miracles by the hands of Paul.

Acts 19:11

Titus

The Man Who Was a Helper and Comforter

The apostle Paul was tired. He had been through hard times. There were fights all around him. He needed to rest. God sent Titus to Paul. Titus took care of Paul. He helped him in many ways. He told Paul all the good news from his friends. Titus comforted Paul.

A Real Hero

1. Ask an adult to take you to see someone who needs to be comforted.
2. Do something nice to help your mom or dad right now.

God . . . comforted us by the coming of
Titus.

2 Corinthians 7:6

Timothy

The Man Who Was a Truth Protector

Timothy was a young preacher. He traveled with Paul. They were close friends. Paul thought of Timothy as his son. Later, Paul wrote a letter to Timothy. He told Timothy to protect the truth of God's Word from false teachers. God gave Timothy important work to do for Him. He was a true hero.

A Real Hero

1. Write a letter to your minister. Ask your minister to protect the truth of God's Word.
2. Sing "The B-I-B-L-E" with someone.

The glorious gospel of the blessed God . . .
was committed to my trust.

1 Timothy 1:11

Other books in this series

My Very First Book of Bible Words

My Very First Book of Lessons

My Very First Book of Bible Prayers